EVERY W

We All Have Issues

Rev/Dr. Marilyn Washington

ABOUT THE AUTHOR

Rev/Dr. Marilyn Washington was born in New Orleans, La., to Cleveland and Neomia Lovincy. One of four daughters, she grew up in a loving family. She is married to Pastor Michael Washington, Pastor of New Vision Outreach Ministries in Donaldsonville, La. Rev. Washington, and her husband has three children, 11 grandchildren, and one greatgrandchild. She is a graduate of Southern University. She worked for 34 years in the public school system serving as a teacher and administrator. She is also an associate minister, praise leader, prayer warrior, women ministry overseer, founder, and New Vision Christian School administrator.

TABLE OF CONTENTS

INTRODUCTION

L ife has a way of taking us in directions we have no desire to go. I laugh now when I think about how fast I wanted to grow up, be a woman, put on my big girl clothes. If I only knew then what I know now. Responsibility will hit like the force of a hurricane and make you want to go back to brighter days. Pain, worry, conscientious living will make you walk on highways you never wanted to drive. People, Lord have mercy; people can bring so much heartbreak and drama in your life that it'll make you cry. In all of the years that I have lived, I've learned that no man, no woman, no boy or girl is worth losing your soul. Lord knows I've had some good days, and I've had some bad days, but every day that I spent with Jesus was a good one.

Every woman God created has a story; every woman has a testimony. Every Woman can help somebody. Every Woman can do some good. Every Woman can do God's work. Instead of watching *"The Young and the Restless,"* " *Scandal,"* and all the other shows that distract us from our fundamental purposes in life, we need to pray, praise, and worship daily to do some good. God knows the secrets of every heart. He knows every thought that goes through your mind before you even think it. God's Women are intelligent, willing, spiritual beings who operate in the gifts, not the gutter. They don't depend on the physical but lean totally on the spiritual. Every woman's purpose is to testify to Jesus, give Him praise in all things, and be ye doers of the Word. That is a big job, but we are well able to do it if we stay focused on the mission and not the mess. We are equipped with heavenly armor to do battle and win. No one ever said it would be easy, but we know it is worth it.

This book, Every Woman, describes the experiences of a group of women living in a small town called Heartsville. Heartsville is your typical country town. There are few businesses, lots of lands, and plenty of gossips to go around. New Vision, the church where the women meet, is in the city's heart. This group of women has been together, as a group, for five years and has done many great things for the community but especially for the women and children. They have had and continue to have their share of troubles individually and collectively. Even though they have done a lot of work to benefit others, having the desire to do good is not enough to keep Satan out. Satan shows up for every meeting, puts himself on the agenda, and causes all manner of problems.

Every woman has issues. We can hide our problems, lie about them, ignore them, magnify them, minimize them, but in most cases, we can't eliminate them, so we must live with and through them. It is always the Prayer of a Christian woman that she can pleasingly deal with her issues to God. If we are fortunate, there are times that God will allow us to walk through our storms with assistance from our sisters in Christ, who work with us in our daily journey.

Every woman needs a support system. It may be one individual or five. Having someone to share with you in your time of need is truly a gift from

God. Knowing that someone cares and is willing to share their time and talents with you is truly a blessing. We are better together. But how can we walk together if we cannot agree?

The stories that you will read about in this book are true. The names have been changed to provide privacy to those that had the experiences and wanted to share their stories. God Bless All of You.

1

WHY AM I HERE?

Getting women to work together is serious business but a problematic endeavor. Men work together daily and usually don't have the problems and drama that many female workers experience. Women are emotional and tend to bring a lot of drama to situations that men sometimes ignore. Even though the endeavor is not always successful, we still have women willing to give their all while trying to help others in need. The group of women from New Vision was one such group. Though far from perfect, they devoted time, energy, and heart to do something for others. They knew the odds of staying together and working as a group historically were not popular, but they still chose to fight the norms and prove that you can do good for others with due diligence and God's help.

It's meeting night for the Women of Vision. We find them coming together in their usual place, the church meeting center, and about to start their meeting.

"We've been meeting here now for over seven years. That's a long time," says Ruth to the Group. " Yes, it is," replies Naomi." We've done some good during that time too." "Amen to that sister," Mary adds. "Many women have been encouraged by what we do here. We're making a difference". "We made some mistakes too, don't forget that." Stacy sarcastically interjects. "Why do you always have to bring up the negative?" Marilyn yells at Stacy.

" I'm not being negative; I just believe if you forget your mistakes, you are going to repeat them," Stacy throws back to Marilyn.

Naomi interrupts the banter and says, " I understand what she means. If you don't face your failures, you don't learn from the experience. We have corrected many of our mistakes. We're not perfect, but I think the Lord is pleased. We've helped women who needed help, And that's the important thing to remember". Stacy responds by saying, " Well, I've never had to repeat anything; I learn the first time."

Marilyn quickly responds to Stacy, " OK little Jesus, unfortunately, most of us didn't learn the first time. It took us a little longer before we got it. You are always trying to act like you're perfect."

" Perfect, ha ha, no, not perfect, but I did it the right way. I got a husband, a job, we bought a beautiful home, and then we had two children, a boy, and a girl. both of which are successful". Marilyn responds in kind, "Yea, right." " What do you mean, yeah right? You never want to speak well of my children. I think you're jealous." The women continue to stare as the two of them go back and forth. Marilyn did not miss her turn and responded, "Jealous? Of What? You are so delusional. I haven't had a drink in 7 years, but when I'm dealing with you, all I can think about is Vodka, Vodka, Vodka".

Ruth finally has had enough and shouts to both of them, " OK Ladies, ok, ok, that's not why we are here tonight. We're here to give God Glory and figure out what we can do to help someone else. Not for the two of you to tear each other apart. Every time we come here, it's the same thing with you two. It's getting to the point that on meeting nights, I don't want to come". Two more ladies, Dora and Barbara, enter at this time and bid good evening to everyone.

"How's everybody doing?" says Barbara" It's getting chilly out there." Dora crosses the room to hang her coat, and the room remains silent for the moment. Putting her jacket down, she moves to the table and gets a seat. She notices that everyone is quiet. "Did we miss something?" she whispers.

" No, but you're right. It is chilly outside. That's why I came a little early to warm the place up a little. I put the coffee on if anybody wants any", says Ruth.

Naomi gets up and moves to the table before any bickering can occur. She announces, " I baked some cookies. I know you girls have a sweet tooth. So I brought enough for everybody. Help yourselves." "Thank you, girl.

You know I got a sweet tooth." Marilyn laughs ".

" Not for me; I have to watch my figure," declares Stacy.

"You better since nobody else is watching it" Marilyn laughs and looks at the others. Stacy is upset and responds, " I don't believe you said that. I am in good shape".

At this point, Ruth screams, "Ladies, Please, if we didn't know better, we would think you were enemies. Let's get on to why we are here". Marilyn shrugs and says," I'm sorry, I apologize. You're right. That's not why we are here".

Dora speaks for the first time and says, "Every time we have a meeting, the two of you are at each other's throat. What's going on?" Stacy responds with many attitudes, "She's Just jealous of me. She always has been".

" What?" Marilyn confronts her and begins to speak when Ruth turns to face her and says to her, "If you don't mind, I got this." Marilyn covers her mouth and does not mutter a sound.

Ruth, the group leader, obviously upset, takes over the conversation at this point and says, " OK, let's get this out of the way. What is it you think she is jealous of"? Stacy takes a deep breath, looks at the group, and says," She's jealous of my job, my house, my husband, our success, our children. Look at where she lives in that run-down trailer park. While we have a beautiful two-story home, cars, boat, and a thriving business". Stacy snarls at Marilyn. Before Marilyn can respond, Dora responds to Stacy.

" Baby, let me tell you something. Thank God for your job, thank him for your house, thank him for your husband and children. I pray that everything continues to go well. But a job, a big house, cars and a boat in and of itself can't make you happy. Just because you got a big house doesn't mean it's a home. Joy is not measured by how much stuff you got. If you're not having any problems now, fall on your knees and thank God because either we're in trouble, coming out of trouble, or getting ready to go into trouble. The Bible says in this life. We will have some trials and tribulations. If you're not using that big house and a big job in the service of the Lord, it's not worth a thing anyway. Pray, baby; bad days are coming; we all have trials and tribulations. Don't brag on you; brag on what God has done to and through you."

"Amen, praise the Lord, she told you." Marilyn gets in another jab at Stacy. Stacy rolls her eyes at Marilyn, but she does not take the bait; she remains quiet.

Ruth clears her throat and says, " Can we get back to business? I appreciate all of you for your commitment to this group. I know it has not been easy. If we are to move forward, we need to stay prayed up. Satan has a way of trying to separate us. It's a tactic to get us off course. Right now, I can see him working on the inside of this group. He is trying to cause strife among us. Right now, he is causing us to be upset with each other. When we get upset, disgusted, and disillusioned, all of the good work we plan to do is over. No one wins but satan. I don't know about you, but I refuse to let him win."

" Yea, you're right about that. Mary says, " Satan knows how to separate women, make us argue and fight over stupid stuff while the real things we are supposed to be doing go undone. When will we come together and use our strength and power for good? Lord Have Mercy. We could move mountains if we could come together".

"Amen to that," says Dora. Before anyone could say or do anything else, there was a loud, startling knock at the door. Everyone turns to the sound, wondering who or what was causing it. "Can someone get the door?" Ruth ask. Marilyn jumps up immediately and responds, "I will." She swiftly moves to the door, and standing there is a young woman that appears to be about fifteen years old. She is dressed in tight shabby clothing, high-heeled boots, lots of makeup, and hair reaching her back. Marilyn smiles at the young lady and says, "Hi, Can I help you?" The young lady responds angrily, " Can I come in?" Staying in character, Marilyn continues to smile and says ", Of course, you can." The young lady pushes past Marilyn and enters the room. Entering the room, she appears to be investigating every aspect of the room and the people in the room. She looks around from one person to the next without uttering one word. Everyone's attention is focused on her as she is on them. Finally, Neomia gets up, extends her hand to the young lady, and says, " Hi, how are you today? Can we help you"? The young lady refuses to shake her hand but again angrily responds,

"Why yall looking at me like that? I must want something. I'm here". Mary, the queen of calm, responds, " I'm sorry, sweetheart. we're not trying to annoy you, just trying to help you if we can?". The young lady again looks them over and appears to have changed her mind. She yells at them," You know what, I made a mistake coming here. I'm going about my business" and begins to walk out. Naomi immediately moves toward the young lady and pleads with her, " Wait, Wait, listen, I'm sorry for whatever we said that upset you. That was not our plan. We are here to help women, any woman with a need, and we can help you if you let us. We don't mean any harm. We are here for you. So, if there is something we can do for you, please don't go, let us help. Please come and sit down." Once again, the young woman glares around the room and finally says, " Alright, if yall want to help."

Ruth now makes her way over to the young lady. She does not extend her hand, remembering how upset it made her earlier, but instead, she says, "my name is Ruth, myself along with these ladies work to help anyone that we can. How can we help you today."

"OK, lady, here's what I need. I live on the street. I do my business on the street. I need some food and some money to buy rubbers. Can yall help me with that?" Shocked to their cores, no one immediately responds. Before anyone else could respond, Stacy pipes up and says to the young lady,

" No, we ain't buying you no rubbers. You selling yourself and still ain't got no money". The young lady snarls at Stacy, " Look, lady, I didn't come here to hear no preaching. I know what I do. I know where I do it, and I know how to do it. I came here because somebody told me yall help women. They lied. Yeah, what you are looking at?" she says to Barbara; I'll take your man too." Barbara said not a word but covered her mouth in amazement.

Naomi again approaches the young lady to reason with her. "Wait a minute, Sweetheart, we do have food. And we would love you to sit and eat. We'll get it for you. Somebody, please get her a plate." Still suspicious of her surroundings, she sits, constantly looking around at everyone. Someone brings her a plate, and she hungrily begins to shove food in her mouth as if she has not eaten for days.

Stacy had heard and seen enough, gets up, gathered her purse, and said to the ladies, " Well, if you all are going to feed and entertain Ms. Thing, I'm leaving. She doesn't even know how to say thank you. I think yall need to throw her out so she can go back to wherever it is she came from."

"Old lady, you know what you can do for me?" "Yes," Stacy responds, " I do. I can get you out of my eyesight." Marilyn yells to Stacy, "Why don't you just shut up?" "Oh, I'll do better than that; I'll leave." Stacy retrieves her purse and coat. " See ya, wouldn't want to be ya," Stacy yells to the young lady as she leaves. The young lady screams after her, " Love you too, Sister Fake." She then turns to the remaining ladies and says, " So, who else is going with her? I know yall can't stand to look at me. I can tell by the look on your faces. But yall the saved people. Want to help a poor little girl like me. Yall don't have a clue. I am sitting here in your cozy little room. Anybody in here knows anything about real-life???? Yall living in a fantasy".

Naomi responds to the young lady, " That's not true. I don't know why you are doing what you do. And I wish you weren't because I don't believe it's safe for you, but I would never talk down or bad about you. I have been raised to Love, everybody. These women are good, and they do the best they can. We will help you as much as we can."

" So I guess I should say thank you." the young lady says. "You're welcome," said Naomi.

" How old are you, baby?" asked Ruth. She answers loudly, "I'm not a baby. I am 18 years old". "So you're 18 years old. What's your name, sweetheart?"

The young lady stands and yells, "You don't need to know my name. What are you trying to find out? What are you going to do report me to the cops?" "No, I would never do that?" Mary cries, "Where are you from? Can we do something to help you get home"?

The young lady hilariously laughs out loud, " Why would I want to go home? I ran away from there.

" Dora says, " You are telling us that you're happy with where you are right now?"

"Happy? Happy, are you serious? Is anybody in this world happy? Do you think it was happiness in the house I came from? Do you think I ran away because I was happy? No, I left to get away from my loving family. Away from my mother, who married a monster. My horrible, horrifying stepfather that I could no longer take. Every night since he married her, he entered into my room and raped me". The woman in the room gasped loudly, stung by the words coming out of her mouth, but she continued. " Every night he was threatening me that if I told anybody, he would kill me. And you want to know the best part. When I told my mother, she did not believe me when I spoke to the woman who brought me into the world. My loving mother said, "He wouldn't do that." She called me a liar and accused me of trying to break up her marriage. So, I left. So that's what I should run back to? Yall sound crazy. There is no way I'm going back there."

"What about other family members? Is there anywhere you could go"? Barbara asked.

"No, lady. Nowhere!!". She puts on her coat. Turns to the ladies and says, "Now thank you for the food and the interrogation. Can anyone spare me $5.00?". Everyone looks at each other but remains quiet". Neomia again pleads with her, " Won't you let us try and find somewhere for you to stay?"

" Lady, I already told you no. Anybody going to loan me $5"? Nobody speaks, so she starts to walk out. Again, Neomia jumps and says, " I'll give you $5.00. But I would like you to made me a promise. If you ever need us, please come back. If you change your mind, please come back.

"Ok," she says as she grabs the money and runs from the room.

"That breaks my heart," cried Barbara

" Mine too," Mary sniffs quietly, " But for the Grace of God that could be my daughter."

"I can't believe that any woman would take the word of a man against her daughter," Marilyn exclaims with a heartbroken look on her face.

Ruth takes a deep and says, "The truth is it happens every day. In this community and communities like it all over the world. I wish I could say this is an isolated incident, but it is not. This young lady is one of the thousands out there on the street. I pray she comes back. We need to pray for her. All of us. Keep her lifted us that the Lord will keep her safe"

"We need to give thanks for good mothers." Mary says, " We tend to take our parents, both mothers, and fathers, for granted. We know they're there, and we expect they'll always be there. But unfortunately, everybody does not have a good mother. I thank God for my mother". The 'me too' went around the room. Each woman is now thinking about their own life and experiences with their mother.

Suddenly the door opens, and Stacy walks in. " I'm back. I saw the bag lady leave. How disgusting was that? I'm so glad she's gone." Everyone stares at her as Ruth approaches her. No one, not even Marilyn, says a word. Ruth gets close to her and begins speaking loud enough for everyone in the room to hear. " Hear me and hear me well. We are here to help women. All women, pretty women, ugly women, smelly women, fat women, skinny women, black women, white women, any woman. If you don't want to be a part of that, you should leave now. We don't shame women; we don't laugh at women; we do our best to help them. That is our mission. You acted very ugly toward that young lady ".

" Ugly toward her; she was rude and ungrateful," Stacy replies.

"Anyone can see that child is hurting and needs help. I don't think that this type of work is for you," Ruth says as she walks away from her.

"OK, Ok, I apologize. I won't do it again," Stacy exclaims

" I don't think you understand, what we do here affect people's lives. This is serious. This is not a game".

" I'm sorry, It won't happen again. I didn't mean any harm," Stacy now pleads as everyone continues to look at her.

"I think we ought to put her out," Marilyn turns to Neomia and says. "Kick her to the curb."

"Alright, Alright. We need all the help we can get. I am not for kicking anybody to the curb. all of us make mistakes. Obviously, Stacy made a mistake". Looking at Stacy, Dora continues, "If you are serious, I think you should stay, and we should move forward. If it happens again, then we need to take action, but for now, can we move on"?

"I agree", most respond.

"Is everybody ok with this? I still think we ought to put her out, but if yall want to give her another chance, OK. I don't really agree with it, but I'll go along for the good of the group," Marilyn said while looking directly into the eyes of Stacy.

Ruth intervenes, "Thank you, Marilyn. Anybody else needs to address this matter?" Nobody speaks up, so she says, I think we have done all we can do for today. It's been quite a day. Let's go home, continue in prayer, and return next week with a new and more vital determination. Again, thank you, ladies.

Ruth walks away shaking her head. Why are we here? She wonders. Why has God put us here? Why am I here? What is my purpose? Why has God put me here at this precise moment? I know that God has his hands on me. I know that I am in His Will. I know that I want to serve him. I know what the Great Commission says. Some days our vision is so clear and others, after dealing with situations like today, look cloudy. Today, I was here to help a young lady who needed help. I need to continue to pray for her.

God, I know I'm here because you willed it so. Bless me Lord with the strength and courage to do what needs to be done according to your will. Amen

2

TIME TO STOP HIDING

I t was 5:30 p.m. Time to get things ready for our weekly meeting. I arrived at the building at about 5:15. Everything was quiet. I moved to the radio and turned it to the KKAY radio station. The sound of gospel music began to play one of my favorite songs: 'Break Every Chain.' I was in a good mood. I got everything set for the meeting and decided to sit and enjoy the music. I had at least a half-hour before everyone arrived.

I pulled out my Bible and began reading while the music was still playing. I was so involved I didn't hear when the first person entered the room. It was not until she tapped me on the shoulder that I realized that I was no longer alone.

"Hi Ruth, I love your music. Nothing like a good old hymn. How are you today?" Naomi said, smiling. "I'm doing OK, Neomia. Listening to that music and reading my bible is always good for me. How are things with you?" "

I'm OK, just tired. I can't wait until I retire. I'm going to get some profound rest." "Don't be so sure," Ruth responds "retirement is not quite what people expect. I retired and went back to work. When you retire and are on a fixed income, that can be hard. Prices keep going up, but your income remains the same. Finances can get stretched when funds are limited. If anything comes up, any emergency, you're in trouble. To make it, I had to do some part-time work. Every little bit helps".

"I guess I'll have to wait until my turn come because I need a serious break. I want some time to do nothing. I want to sit, drink coffee and read my newspaper. I want to watch TV at night as late as I want and not worry about what time I have to get up. I want to get up when I feel like it and not when I have to". " I understand what you're saying. I was there a little while myself. I know the feeling. But my reality was, I couldn't make it on what was coming in. I hope your situation works for you better than it was for me."

"Well, here come the ladies. Good evening, everybody. I got coffee if anybody wants any". A few of the ladies get coffee, and others stand talking to each other. Gradually everyone moves to the table and takes a seat. When everyone is seated, I stand and begin the meeting the same way I usually do by thanking everyone for coming ." I realize that all of you are busy. But I thank you for coming out to try and help somebody else. God knows there are a lot of women who need help. Most women have no one they can talk to. It's terrible when you have nobody at all. The book of Titus tells us that we should reach out to help young women. It tells us that we should be role models for them to look to and see what they need to do in the service of God. We should show them how to be good mothers, good housekeepers, good wives, and serve in the church. They should be able to come to us, but we must let our lights shine. We must be doing it right ourselves so that they would feel comfortable to come and talk to me, or you, or anyone of us.

" You're so right, Ruth. We're losing young women every day. I read about a young lady in our community just last week who committed suicide. Two small children left without a mother. She went on Facebook and said she had no friends and no one to talk to. No one reached out to help her, and she took that as a sign that nobody loved her. How awful is that?" Barbara said with tears rolling from her eyes.

" I think they need to get off Facebook. Too many opinions on there. Too many people are trying to find themselves. It's the wrong place to be looking for love, companionship, and answers to life's problem". Dora explained.

Marilyn says, " Look, Facebook is not the issue. We are forming the wrong relationships. On Facebook, people try and get you to believe that they are who they are not. Too many fake people. We have to build relationships with people we know. We don't have time to be at war with one another, on Facebook, or even face to face. We need to get our face in the book God's book, the Bible".

"You're right about that, I agree," says Mary.

"I agree with you, but there is only so much you can do. People hide out and lie to the public to make themselves look good. The truth is not always pretty, but eventually, it will come out.

Look, ladies, In the last three months, we have been able to talk with over 16 young women and help them in some way or another. Again, I'd like to thank all of you because, without you, we would not have been able to do any of this. But tonight, is another night, and we don't know what will come up before it's over. However, I know that at least one will show up tonight. Neoma, please tell them everything we know about this young lady that has called and said she would show up tonight," Ruth asks.

"I don't have that much info on her, but here's what I do know. She's been calling on and off for about three months. She is married and has at least one child. I can tell when she calls that she's been crying. She keeps saying she's going to come in, but she never set a time or a date until now. I don't know what happened, but this morning she called and said she would be here tonight".

"Naomi, what time did she say"? Dora asked. "She said about six-thirty. That's just a few minutes from now. But let me add this, I think her husband has been beating her. She didn't tell me that, but that's the impression I got".

That statement angers Stacy, and she says, "I don't know how a woman can be so stupid to let a man beat them. Why don't they leave"?

Barbara responds with, "that's easy to say, but it's not that easy to do."

"Yes, it is," Stacy announces, " just put one foot in front of the other and keep moving."

Dora moved toward Stacy and said, " Baby, look, it's never that easy. If you have never walked in another woman's shoes, don't be so quick to judge her. All of us were raised differently; you don't know what that child had to live with when she was growing up. You don't know what she's going through daily. Especially if she has children, listen; a woman will go through hell to do what she can for her children. Even let a man hit her. Do I agree with that? No way, but it's a terrible situation, and when and if she walks in here tonight, don't start by telling her just put one foot in front of the other and go. We need to listen to what she says and not judge her. There is too much judging going on. There's a reason God gave us two ears and one mouth. He wanted us to listen more".

Dora is so right. Please, Please, listen to what she is saying. That's very important. I was in a situation where I was getting beat for ten years. Yes, me, Barbara Harmon; I kept saying I would leave. Every time I said it, things got a little better before they got much worse. I stayed there for ten years....10 long years getting black eyes and bruises in places you wouldn't imagine. Everybody told me I should have left. And I knew I should, but I just couldn't. I lied over and over to people. I was embarrassed. I hid as much as I could for as long as I could. Not until the night he held a gun to my head, pull the trigger, and I passed out. When I came through, I was lying on the floor with my four-year-old, putting a wet towel on my head calling my name. Fortunately, the barrel was empty. That night changed my life. I finally, finally realized what was happening to me. God had given me another chance. After that, my mind was made up; I planned how to get out for weeks. I couldn't pack a suitcase because if he saw one, he would be suspicious. I packed my clothes and my children's clothes in plastic bags. A little bit at a time. It took me over a month to get everything I needed in place. Thank God I had my sister who helped me. Five weeks after he pulled that gun on me, I finally had my opportunity to get out of there. One night, he came home drunk, as usual, he was mad about everything. He told me to fix him some food, and when I did, he threw it in my face. When I complained, he slapped me. I didn't say a word; I didn't want to aggravate him further. Eventually, after torturing me further, he went to bed and fell asleep. When I realized he was sleeping, I got busy and got us out of the house. I gathered our little bags I had been packing over the last few weeks. I didn't even take the car because I didn't want him coming after me for a car. I didn't go to my momma's house because I knew that was the first place he would go. The first place I went was to the police department. I cried my heart out, explaining to them what had happened. The police department said they would go to pick him up. Taking pictures of the bruises on my face and body was so embarrassing. I felt stupid. Once contacted the social worker brought us to Catholic Charities. They helped us by putting us up in a hotel room. I was told later that the police went to our home and found my husband drunk and asleep. They put him in jail. The following day he told the police that I had hit him and that's why he had hit me. He got out of jail and, just like I thought he would, he went looking for me. He contacted all my friends and went straight to my mother's house looking for me. No one gave him any help. We were able to get out of town to my sister's house. I knew that was one place he would not come because she was an FBI agent. He never liked her and knew she would not hesitate to put him away. Finally, we were free. He never made contact with me after that. When I filed for divorce three years later, he never showed up in court, and I got it automatically.

It was so hard making a way for my children and me. I moved here, 10,000 miles away, and I've been here ever since. That was 15 years ago, and sometimes I still fear that he'll come back on me. But I know that he would have killed me if I had not done what I did. I thank God I got out, but I see women doing just what I did every day. And I feel for them, but don't you think it is easy for one minute. That was the hardest thing I have ever done in my life".

The sisters all began hugging and encouraging Barbara. " Why didn't you tell us?" "I told Neomia and Ruth. They told me not to share until I was comfortable sharing. Tonight, was my time. I can relate to this young lady tonight, So I thought it important enough to say now".

"Thank you, Barbara, for sharing with us. Ecclesiastes says there is a time for everything. Tonight, was your time". Naomi finished.

Stacy seems to be uninterested in what was being said and shared, she stands, gathering her purse, and says, "Well, maybe I should leave because I really can't relate to this case tonight. It's making me uncomfortable."

Ruth quickly responds, " If you're not comfortable, I agree with you. Because this young lady, if she comes, needs our undivided attention. If she comes, we must be all on one accord to offer her some help. However, it's already past the time she was supposed to get here. She may not come".

" Let's give her a few minutes. Anybody wants coffee or cookies ?" Naomi asked.

"You know me," Marilyn smiles, "I love cookies. Yea, I'll take some coffee and some cookies".

Everyone settles down and begins socializing. A few minutes later, everything goes silent when there's a knock on the door. At the same time,

Stacy has gathered her purse and coat and is preparing to leave. **As she goes down toward the door to exit, a young lady walks in**. She says "Hi" without looking up and keeps moving toward the door. " Hi, Can we help you? Ruth ask.

" Yes, I'm the one who has been calling," she says. "Oh, please come in,"

Neomia says" we've been waiting on you."

Stacy hears the young lady's voice as she reaches the door; she turns around, in shock, and asks, "Melanie, what are you doing here?"

The young lady looks at her in amazement, recognizing who she is, and responds, "Mom, what are you doing here?"

"This is the group I told you I joined, the Titus Woman Group."

Melanie looks confused and tells her mother, "You told me you joined a group of gossiping old women trying to mind other people's business."

"No, you must have misunderstood me," Stacy says as she moves toward her daughter.

" No, isn't this the group you joined because at work you had to give some type of community service to get your raise, mom?".

" Melanie, that's beside the point. What are you doing here? They said that the young lady coming tonight was in trouble".

Ruth places herself between the two of them and tells Melanie, "please come and take a seat."

"No, I don't think so," Melanie says. "I don't need another group of people making fun of me and trying to ruin my life. I made a mistake; I think I need to go".

" Listen, Melanie; I don't know what your mother has told you. But here is a safe place for you; we would not dare try and tell you what to do. Our job is to love you and help you. However, you want us to do it. We will do nothing you don't want us to do or say anything to anybody. We are only here to help. Please stay, please". Ruth pleaded

Looking at her mother cautiously, she says, "OK, I'll stay a little while."

Ruth takes her by the hand and leads her to a chair to sit and says to her, "can I get you some coffee or something else to drink?" "No," she whispers, "I'm OK."

Stacy comes over to her daughter and once again questions her, " I don't understand. Why are you here? You have a lovely big house, a good job, a handsome husband with a good job...

"And a husband that beats me on the regular," she screams at her mother.

" What are you talking about? Your husband is a lawyer. He's good to you.

I've seen you two together".

"All a show, mother, all of that is a show. That big, beautiful house you're talking about is not a home for me; it's a torture chamber. I wouldn't say I like it. I hate it. I'd rather live under a bridge than be in that house".

"Melanie, what are you talking about? You have a wonderful husband, two beautiful children, a good education, and a good job. You must be kidding?"

"Kidding mother? Is that what you called it when daddy hit you?"

Backing away from her daughter, apparently in shock, she responds, "What are you talking about. You have a good father".

"Yes, he was good to us, but that didn't stop him from hitting you. Didn't you think we knew? We heard him so many nights. We heard you crying late at night when you thought we were sleeping. We saw the bruises you tried to hide; we saw all of it mom".

" Melanie, be quiet; I don't know what you're talking about."

" Why are you lying? To look good for the neighbors. To keep pretending that everything is perfect in your little world? I tried to be like you mom, just pretend that nothing was happening, that it was worth it to have a big house, big car, and credit cards. IT'S NOT WORTH IT; IT'S NOT WORTH IT. I can't take it anymore; I just can't,". she says now, crying openly. Finally, Stacy runs to hug her daughter repeatedly, saying, "I'm sorry, I'm soo sorry. I never wanted to hurt you all. You don't deserve to be beaten. I'm sorry I set that example for you. I'm going to help you. I'll do whatever you need me to do. I am truly sorry, Baby". Slowly Stacy stands and faces the other ladies. With tears rolling from her eyes, she falls into a chair and begins crying uncontrollably. The ladies do their best to comfort Stacy and her daughter. After a few minutes, Stacy stands and begins walking back and forth and speaking to the ladies and her daughter.

"I apologize to all of you. I've been living a lie. I've been living this lie for so long that it has become my reality.

My daughter's right: My husband has been beating me for years. I just...I Just....took it. I don't know why. I fought to get a good job, I fought to get a good position and salary on that job, but when it came to him, I never fought. After the first time he hit me, he apologized and said it would never happen again. he sent me flowers and a new piece of jewelry. I thought he must be very sorry and I was sure it would never happen again. In less than a month, it had happened again. He told me that things at work were not going well and that he was under a lot of pressure. Like before I got flowers and a new diamond ring. After that, there were more apologies.

I thought it was a small price to pay for how we lived. We were not in the project; we were not in a trailer; we lived in a beautiful two-story house. People always commented on how beautiful the furniture was and how nice it was, But nobody knew what happened behind closed doors. At least I thought nobody did. (Looks at her daughter) I thought my children were happy. I had no idea they knew what was going on. But I was wrong; look at what I did to my daughter. I would never wish what I've been going through on my worst enemy".

Marilyn goes to Stacy and hugs her, saying, " Stop blaming yourself. You did nothing wrong. You're the victim, not him. You did what you thought you had to do. Now you need to do what's right for you".

" Thank you, Marilyn; I've been so mean to you. I was jealous of you. You live in a doublewide. But you were always so happy. I couldn't stand it. I wanted you to be miserable like me. I thought I had it all. I'm so sorry".

"No problem. I have my share just like anybody. I give God Praise that things are as well as they are. We are here for you, we'll help you get through this".

" I owe an apology to all of you. Stacy declared, " I've been a real pain."

Ruth walks over to Stacy, hugs her, and tells her, "You don't owe us anything. That's not why we are here. All honor goes to God. Sit down, sit down beside your daughter, join hands with your daughter and let us pray". They all join hands, and the words to the first song I heard earlier, Break Every Chain, rolled through my mind. Indeed tonight, we needed him to Break Every Chain. Dora prayed for the group, and I turned to Stacy and her daughter and asked the age-old question, "Where do you go from here"?

Stacy goes over, takes her daughter's hand in hers, and says to her daughter, "We'll take care of each other. Melanie is coming home with me, and we're going to work it out. I promise you big changes are on the horizon. Thank you for all your help". Stacy and her daughter leave the building clinging to each other. Everyone looks around, not knowing exactly what to say as they exit. Ruth looks at the group of women lovingly. So grateful for them, she says, "Thank you, ladies, let's go home." Everyone agrees and begins gathering their things and begins to exit the building.

Three months later.as they are in the midst of their meeting there is a knock at the door.

Marilyn gets up to answer the door. After opening the door she turns around smiling and says "Look who's here It's Stacy".

Stacy comes in and hugs all the Ladies. She stands smiling and says It's so good to see you all. I missed you all. I wanted to come by and let you all know what has been going on.

Ruth takes her hands and say "You know you don't have to tell us anything. We're just happy you're doing ok."

No, Stacy says "that's where you're wrong. I do have to tell you. I lived a lie for a long time. Now I'm standing on the truth. The Bible says that pride is a sin. I've been prideful for too long. I tried keeping all my dirty laundry to myself. Now, I'm free. I'm not afraid to let anybody know what I've been through. If it had not been for you ladies and all the prayer and help you gave me, I know I would not have been able to do it myself. I filed my divorce papers. It was so hard because I still had all the stuff I was losing on my mind. I wanted my house; I wanted all my clothes; I wanted my new car. But I came to a place where he could have it all. All of a sudden, it did not matter. He could have the house; he could have the car; he could have all the money; I didn't care. My lawyer thought I was crazy, but for the first time in my life, all I wanted was Jesus. I prayed day and night. Everyday. I still do.

"So, you lost everything?" Ruth asked " I feel so bad for you.'"

Stacy smiled, "Don't feel bad for me. I didn't lose anything. God fixed it. My husband was afraid I would press charges against him. As a lawyer, he would lose his license if he was convicted as being a wife beater. So he offered me everything, the house, my car, and half of his money. God fixed it. I didn't lose a dime. I got double for my trouble"

Hallelujah

Stacy claps her hands and continues. "God fixed it. It's just like the Pastor said. It was a fixed fight. He had settled it before I even got started. Oh, he knows how to work it out All I had to do is put it in his hands

He fixed it all right. he didn't give me what I needed. He gave me more than enough. Now I can help other women with my testimony, but I have a little extra money. So, I'm back, Ladies. But this time for the right reason. I'm here to help in any way you will have me if that's OK with all of you.

"Of course, we'll have you. How's your daughter?"

Oh, she's with me. Stacy says "She had a phone call she was finishing up but she's coming in." At that moment there is a knock on the door and Melanie enters. With a smile on her face she enters and says, "Hi Everybody."

Everyone hugs and greet her.

Marilyn grabs her by the hands and ask, "How are you doing, sweetheart? You look great. "I'm great,' Melanie responds I'm good and my children are doing great too. Neomia goes over to greet her and tells her, " We've been praying for you."

"Thank you, thank all of you." Melanie responds. "I know. I needed it, and I still do. I've come a long way, and I've got a long way to go. Since I saw all of you, my kids and I moved to live with my mom. I didn't want to admit it, but I needed the help. We've been able to help each other. I'm almost finished with my divorce. After that, I can begin to focus on what's next. It's hard. I'm so embarrassed to be in public. I can hear people talking about me as I walk by sometimes

"You can't worry about people" Mary says,." People will talk about you if you do good, and they will talk about you if you do bad. You can't win with people. Keep your head and your heart on, Jesus. That's what's going to get you through."

"I know, and I've been doing that. I started going to my Bible Study again, which has helped me a lot." Stacy responds

Ruth takes her hand and looks her in the eyes and says, " Baby, you will have some good days, and you will have some bad, but take it one day at a time. Every day Thank God for getting through today, and before you know it, you'll find yourself smiling again without even thinking about it."

Melanie, now with tears in her eyes says to the ladies, "In all of this I've learned that hiding issues never help. The longer you hide, the worse they get. I've learned to lean and depend on Jesus. Issues must be confronted. If you push things under the rug all you get is a lumpy rug. I gave my burden to the Lord and I thank God he worked it out. Thank you ladies for praying for me. I Love all of you."

Neomia hugs her and tells her, "we all Love you too.

Stacy stands and says, "we're going to have to leave; we have to pick up the kids from school.

Before we go, I'd like to thank all of you again. I don't know where I would be if you all had not been here for us. The work you're doing here is essential.

Melanie joins her mother and says, "She's right. If you all had not been here. I would probably still be in bondage. We want you all to know we appreciate every one of you for everything you did, every kind word, every deed, and every prayer. She hands an envelope to Ruth. This is a donation from me and my mom. We want to make sure you can continue to reach out to other women who need help. It's not much, but it comes from our hearts.

"Thank you so much. Ruth responds, We love you, girls. Please keep in touch." Stacy smiles and look towards Marilyn, "I'll be here. I want to continue to work with you all. Truthfully this time, if you'll have me. " Marilyn smiles at her and says, I guess we can put up with you a little while longer." Everyone laughs

You know you're welcome here anytime. I know you're in a hurry, but can we pray before you leave.

Three months later, Stacy unexpectedly shows up at the weekly gathering of the Titus Women. Things were slow that night, and the women were sitting around the table having a happy conversation about the upcoming holidays. Everyone was startled when the door opened. They had not heard the knock at the door. Stacy enters with a smile on her face and greets all of the ladies. Everyone was excited to see her as they began getting up from their seats to hug and welcome her. After all the hugs, hellos, and how are you doing, Ruth asks, "How have you been"?

Stacy smiles and says, "for the first time in a long time, I can say I am doing fine. Things have been hard. When I left you, ladies, over three months ago, my life was still evolving. I had no big plan about what to do or how to do it. I prayed and took everything one day at a time. I didn't know what I was going to do. I left here with my mind going 100 mph. I knew the first thing I had to do was to continue to help my daughter and grandchildren as much as I could in their transition. I had to put my issues on hold until I knew she and her children were in a good place. They are doing very well now and I really don't have to babysit them anymore"

That's great news Stacy, Neomia says, "But how are you?"

Well, Stacy begins, "About a month ago, I saw my ex-husband it was the first time since our divorce. I wish I could explain to you how I felt. My emotions were over all the place. I felt love, hate, loneliness, rage, pity, confusion and so many other emotions. When he approached me, I thought I wouldn't know what to say. But as he got closer my common sense started to kick in. He walked up and asked, "how have you been?' I said, "I'm good." As he stood there awkwardly not knowing at this point what to expect from me I realized that this man no longer had any power over me. I was able to look at him as I had not seen him in many years, just a man. At that point my composure was back and I approached him.

I approached him, looked him in the eyes and I said everything I wanted to him for the first time in years. I explained everything that we had been through and how it had affected me.. He looked at me calmly and said, "I knew this day would come. I didn't know when. I know I was wrong, but I just couldn't stop. I'm sorry for everything. Do you think you can forgive me"? I looked at him and saw all the pains of my past. Again I felt the freedom that I had not had in years. I looked at my husband, and I said, "Yes, I can forgive you. I forgive you. I wish you the best, and I hope that you will find peace and happiness. And sincerely I meant every word I had said. I realized then that I had been harboring hate in my heart for him. The hate was weighing me down and when I said those words to him I immediately felt relief. It was finally over. I walked up to him, gave him a hug and walked away.

Over the next few weeks, he tried to convince me to have lunch or dinner with him but that was not about to happen. Last week I got a card from him saying he had moved to Dallas. He wanted me to know where he wanted me to know where he was if we needed something. I gave the card to Melanie and told her to keep it. After all he is her father, and she may want to contact him.

It's a strange feeling when I talk about him. I'm not upset; I'm no longer hurt; it's like a person I never really knew. The important thing is that now I have a life, and I have peace like I have never known as an adult. I have communion with God. I am doing my best to live the way

God wants me to. For the first time in many years, I am happy, and I want to thank you all for what you did for my daughter and me."

"There is no need for thanking us," Ruth says as she hugs Stacy. "God had you right where he wants you at this moment. He orchestrated every move in your life. Now you have a testimony. You've passed the test. Use your testimony to be a witness for Jesus. That's who deserves your Thanks.

"I know you're right." Stacy says, "I thank him daily, and I wanted to ask you, ladies again, I know I said it when I was here with Melanie, that I wanted to come back. But I really wasn't ready then. Now it's different. I feel I can really help. If you would allow me to come back and work with you all, I know it would be different this time."

Marilyn comes around her and says to her, "I knew you would be back, couldn't stay away from me. I know you missed me". She hugs Stacy. "And you're right, I surely did. I missed all of you".

"We would be happy to have you back. We missed you too. Welcome back," Neomia spoke quietly.

After that, they returned to their holiday celebration not concerned about anything but each other. Another day of just being there.

Food for thought: It's time for us to come out of hiding. Hiding our issues only causes more hurt. It delays the inevitable but it does not destroy.

3

IS THIS LOVE?

E very day we awake, we behold a new day that we have never seen or experienced before. Sometimes we feel unprepared to deal with what comes up during the day. There is always a plethora of emotions to deal with. Every day we deal with people, situations, and circumstances that causes us to become emotional and sometimes change the course of our day. Let's just face it-women are emotional. Controlling our emotions can be hard work, especially for our young people. Total control comes with experience and determination. When we let our emotions control us, we find ourselves in situations that can quickly go out of control and not necessarily positively or effectively. Love is one of those emotions that can turn our worlds upside down. Sometimes, we're willing to do anything to get love, experience love, and keep love. Unfortunately, we can love and not be loved.

"' Leave me alone!! Let me go!" someone was screaming. I couldn't see who it was, but it sounded like someone was fighting. I ran to the door. I could see a group of people moving toward me, but I could not tell who they were nor what they were doing. I stepped out the door, and as they got closer, I could see Barbara, one of our members, pulling someone. I saw Mary, another member, pulling the same person in the next few seconds. Whoever it was, they were still yelling, "let me go, let me go, I say." As they got closer to the door, they recognized me and screamed, "Open the door." I ran ahead and held the entrance to the building open. As I held the door open, I finally got to see what they were doing. They were pulling a young woman through our front doors. Evident to me was the fact that she was not coming willingly. They got her through the doors and pushed her into a chair. I got the door closed, followed them inside, and asked, "What's going on?" Before they could answer me, the young lady again is yelling to them to leave her alone.

Barbara glares at her and says, " I'll leave you alone alright. I'll bring you straight to that police car and let them lock you up".

" I don't care. Let them lock me up. When I get out, I'm still gonna beat her butt".

Ruth, totally confused, now looks at Barbara and says, "Look, this is interesting, but who is this young lady? She is here against her will. We don't normally force young girls to come here, so what's going on?" She goes over to the young lady and asks," Who are you going to beat?" "I'm gonna beat Mindy," she screamed.

"Who is Mindy? Can somebody tell me what's going on?" Ruth ask again

"I'm at my wit's end with this girl," Barbara explains. "Stupidity. That's what going on plain stupidity. This is my niece. One of my neighbors called me to tell me she was fighting with a girl. I left my house, where I was getting ready for our meeting. It just so happens that Dora was with me. We were going to walk over here together. We ran out of the house because they were right down the street. When we got there, the police had arrived. They were talking to both, this one, pointing to her niece, was still acting a fool. Thankfully, the policeman that was talking to her was from our church. When I walked up, he asked me did I know her? I said yes, "she's my niece"; He told me that if I could calm her down, they would let her come with me because the other girl would leave with her mom.

She was still running her mouth, but he let us take her anyway. We were closer here than my house, so I thought the best thing was to bring her here. I also thought we could talk some sense into her empty head.

"I don't know; Barbra, don't look like your plan is working. Does she always get so upset?" Marilyn asked.

Exasperated Barbara says, "I don't know what's wrong with her. Lately, she has been getting into trouble for little or no reason. I don't know what started this today. I don't ever remember her fighting before."

"Fight, who were you fighting with, young lady?" Ruth glares at the young woman.

"None of your business, old lady," she snarls at Ruth

"Watch your mouth." Says Dora, "You have no reason to disrespect this woman

"That woman had better stay out of my face. Why am I here anyway? I don't want to be here", the young lady continues to scream.

Barbara screams right back at her, "I don't want you here anymore than you want to be here. I'm trying to help you."

Rolling her eyes at everybody she yells again, "I don't need any help. Just get me out of this dump".

"Why don't you pay attention to what she's trying to tell you?" Mary pleads with her.

"I don't need her to tell me anything". She continues to scream

Ruth now calmly looks at her and says, " That's the problem with you young people, you don't know anything and don't want anybody to tell you anything. OK, tell us what this is all about? Why are you so mad at the whole world? What's his name?

Staring at Ruth she almost calmly says "What?"

Ruth continues to stare her in the eyes and says, "What's his name? I know it's about a man. Who is he? That is what this is all about, right? Some man that you believe you are in love with, what's his name?"

" Yes, he's my boyfriend." She responds calmly for the first time "What you got to do with it, old woman? He loves me, and I love him. What do you know about men anyway? Have you ever had a boyfriend? I doubt that"

Smiling Ruth says, "Listen, don't fool yourself; just because the stove looks like it's cold doesn't mean the pilot light is not on. I know more about men in my little finger than you know in your head. So, what's his name? You may as well tell us, or we'll ask the girl you are trying to beat. I know she'll be happy to tell us."

"Alright, his name is James, and he's my boyfriend. She supposes to be my friend, and she was hitting on him."

And?

"What do you mean, And? "

Ruth stands her ground and says, "So you want to beat somebody up because they were trying to get with your boyfriend?"

"That's right"

"How many women are prepared to beat up?"

"As many as I need to"

"And what would that accomplish?"

The young lady takes a deep breath and says, "She needs to be taught a lesson, and I'm the one who's going to give it to her. She's not going to disrespect me like that."

Toe to toe with her now Ruth says, "Oh, you so bad, you going to beat up everybody? Make them respect you."

"That's right, that's right."

So, Ruth says, "Tell me, what kind of respect was your boyfriend showing while she was trying to hit on him? Was he pushing her away? Was he angry? Was he upset? Or was he enjoying it?"

"You don't know what you're talking about."

Ruth continues not letting up, "Let me ask you something? Where is your boyfriend now? I don't see him here supporting you. Maybe he is with the other girl, what's her name, Mindy?"

"No, he's not with Mindy; he left when the police came because they are always picking on him."

Ruth laughs out loud, "That's what he told you anyway, and you believe him?"

"Yea, I believe him"

Yea, I know you do. You believe everything he tells you. Don't you? Tell me something, sweetheart. Who does your boyfriend live with? Ruth ask.

"He lives with me."

"Where does he work?"

"He's laid off right now"

"Who's taking care of him?" Ruth continues

"I am"

"Who's car is he driving? "My car."

Ruth laughs out loud, "Man, he is respecting you. And you are trying to beat up another girl. It seems to me you ought to be beating yourself up for being so silly "

"What"?

Ruth stares her in the eyes, "Why aren't you demanding respect from him? Why aren't you arguing with him? You're feeding a healthy man, clothing and putting money in his pocket, driving your car, with your gas, and you don't see anything wrong with that picture?"

The young lady stares at Ruth. By now she seems uncertain about what she is saying. "I don't know. I love him, and he loves me."

"If he loved you, Ruth goes on, "you wouldn't have to feed him; he'd be providing you, he wouldn't have to drive your car, he would have his own, you wouldn't have to put money in his pocket. He would be putting money in yours."

"You don't know what you're talking about." She starts to cry

Comforting her with a pat on her back, Ruth says, "Listen, honey, just because he has hair on his chest and wears pants don't make him a man

A real man will give you respect

A real man will provide for you.

A real man has too much pride to let you take care of him

A real man won't let just anybody rub upon him; he's particular about who he rubs against

Little boys play with toys, but real men have put away their childless ways

So, why are you crying? I'll tell you why, Because you know what I'm saying is correct. You may very well love James, but it's evident that James loves James; James is looking out for James, James has it going on for James. And that includes cheating on you and that other girl. You're not dealing with a man, honey. You're dealing with a mouse. All a mouse wants is to get his cheese anyway and as often as he can. He eats, and before you know it, he's out looking for more.

"I know that's right" says Barbara

"You have to think about yourself and your future. Tell me one thing that James has done to help you? One thing that he has done to help you be a better person, one thing he had done to help you move to your next level in life. How many of your bills has he paid? How many nights have you spent at his house? How often has he sent you flowers and taken you out to eat?"

Crying softly now the teenager says "I don't know. We don't do stuff like that. I just love him."

"Don't you like flowers? You don't like going out to eat? "

"Yeah, I like flowers, and yes, I want to eat, but he doesn't have time to do that right now."

"It must be because he's too busy working on his job. He just doesn't have time to order flowers or go out to eat." Barbara says

"I know what yall trying to do. She cries, "But I know James loves me."

"Please, baby girl, tell me how you know he loves you." Barbara Pleads "What is it that he does that screams, I love you?"

"Well, he makes love to me all the time".

"Oh, I see, Now having sex means he love you. And what does that do for him? Does he even use protection?" her aunt ask

"We don't need protection. James says, "If I love him, we don't need protection" Everybody in the room laughs at that.

"Really," Ruth says "And what does James say about you becoming pregnant? Who's going to take care of that child? James? Oh no, he has no job. Where is the child going to live? With James? Oh no, he has no house. Who's going to take care of you when you can no longer work, James? Oh no, he has no job."

"It seems to me you put a lot of confidence in someone who has so little" Dora says.

Ruth lifts her chin with her hand, moves closer to her face and whispers to her, "I know you love James. I understand that, but do you love yourself?"

"Yes, I love me"

"Then how can a beautiful woman like you let a man take advantage of her? He got you paying his rent, he got you buying his food, he got you buying his clothes, he's using your car, how is that loving you? " Ruth continues to whisper as she moves away from her.

It seems she has finally run out of things to say. AS Ruth moves away from her she moves closer to Ruth and says, "I don't know; I'm confused. I don't know what to do."

How does that make you feel? Ruth ask her.

Weakly she responds, " I feel used".

"That's because he is using you, baby. Ruth hugs her, "As hard as it to accept, he is. You have to get yourself together and do what's best for you. Listen, you don't have to make any decisions tonight. But promise me you will think about what you've heard here tonight. I've been young, and I've been in love, and it sometimes seems like it is the only thing that matters. You're young, and believe it or not, you're going to fall in love many other times before you find the one. Love is not something that you should have to pay a person for. True love is freely given. I'm going to give you this chapter to read. It's 1 Corinthians 13. It's called the Love chapter. When you get home promise me you will sit and talk to your aunt about it and get a clear understanding of what it's saying. I think you'll have a clearer picture of what happened today. Will you make that promise to me?

Taking the book she says, "Yes, I will"

Thank you.

You've got a long wonderful life ahead of you. My last piece of advice is that you get to know Jesus. Life is so much better with him. We love you, and we're here for you. Ruth hugs her and for the first time she hugs her back.

She whispers to Ruth, "I'm sorry I was rude to you

"That's ok, "Ruth smiles, "we all have our issues."

She goes over and hugs her aunt telling her how sorry she was.

"That's okay." Barbara says "Are you going to be ok? I am always here for you. Please think about what you heard here today."

"Yea, I'll be ok; I need to learn how to take care of myself." As she turns to leave she ask out loud, "Hey, can I come back and talk to you guys sometimes?"

"Anytime You want." They yelled in unison.

Barbara drops on her seat with the question, "What's wrong with these young ladies? Believing that they have to take care of these young men."

Dora laughs, "I guess I'm old-fashioned in my day that was a man's job. Now the women are hard-working, and the men looking good."

Pinch me, Mary says, "What happened? Am I too old to remember? Did I miss something? What happened to our daughters?"

"That's the way of the world today" Dora Explains." Everybody is casual about everything. Waiting to have sex after marriage in my day meant that I did love you. Today it obviously means just the opposite. If you love me you won't wait. You don't need marriage to seal the deal.. We live in a try it I don't need to buy it time. Norms have changed and our young people are caught up in what the world is doing and not with the things of God. We used to learn about Love at home and in the church. Now they're learning it from Facebook, Instagram, Tick Tok and other social media sites. They're learning from TV because of all the time they spend watching. The problem is that's not love. That's acting. Real Love we know is found in Jesus. What our young people need is a good dose of Jesus. We need to pray with and for them. We must continue to disciple and let the world know who he is."

Neomia groans, "That makes me want to cry. Our young women need to be taught how to love themselves. How to respect themselves. No man is worth losing all your dignity over. But that's what our world has come to".

Ruth stands gathering her things to leave stops and says, "But the one thing I know is that the same God that brought us through will bring these young people through as well. God does not sleep. He knows their hearts and their minds. He still reigns. We must continue to serve him and others. It's going to be ok. Because if we know nothing else we know God Loves Us. Let's go home.

4

OUR CHILDREN

For most mothers, the joy of our lives are our children. We live and breathe for them. The Love of a mother is a force to be reckoned with. Mothers love deep and they love hard.

Ruth has been mulling over these ideas about children for a long time. Many nights while meeting with the other ladies, she remained silent. She was not ready to share her story. She felt that sharing her story made her incapable of being a good mother at this point in her life.. How many nights had she been the strong one? The leader? She was the voice of reasoning for this group. What would they think of her when she told them she, too, had issues. Would they laugh? Talk about her behind her back? She could not figure out what they would say or do, but she knew tonight would be her night to share. The last few days had forced her to her knees. She had cried herself sick. She was tired of hiding and feeling guilty about things she had never done. So as she prepared for the women, she mentally prepared herself. She puts a smile on her face, pats her hair into place, and says to herself, "It is what it is."

Before Ruth has time to do anything else, the ladies file in, saying their good evening and carrying on conversations of small talk to each other. Every meeting for this group is like a family reunion. Everyone is happy to see the others. The smile on their faces makes it a comfortable atmosphere to be in. They all gather around the large oval table in the center of the room. After a few moments, they all turn their attention to Ruth. She smiles and asks if anyone wants coffee. No one wished to have coffee, so she turned back to the group. She calls the meeting to order and thanks everyone for coming as she usually does. She then asks Neomia to give them a report of the last meeting. After receiving the information, she calls for the agenda for the night. Naomi looks at the schedule and says, "We only have two things on the agenda. One is our fundraiser, and the other only says children; I don't know what that's about." OK", Ruth says, "let's talk first about the fundraiser. Dora, what do we need to know about the fundraiser?"

Dora grabs her notebook, looks over her notes, and says," not too much tonight. Everything is right on target. We have another month to get ready, but everyone has done what they were assigned to do up to this point. It's been a lot of hard work, but I think it will be a great success. Two weeks before the event, we need to come back and figure out our final steps."" Thanks Neomia, you've done a great job as the leader of this fundraiser. We appreciate all that you've done." The other ladies agreed and told her so.

Naomi looks at her notes and says, "that takes care of the fundraiser. Who put our children as our 2nd topic of discussion?" As she looked around, everyone was quiet, and suddenly Ruth said, "that was me. I wanted to talk to you ladies about something that I have been struggling with."

" You, Ruth," says Mary, "Are you having problems?"

"Of course, she's not having problems; Ruth always has her stuff together.

Don't be silly." Marilyn says.

Neomia senses something in the atmosphere, "Why don't yall let her speak? What's on your mind, Ruth?"

"Well, I don't know where to start. Most of you know I lost a son. When I lost my son, I thought I would lose my mind. My son was my life. Not being married, I dedicated all my time to him. We were so close. We would do everything together. I was his mother and his father. My child was always so happy, so full of life. When he died, it was as if all the lights around me went out. He was only 20 years old, a student in college, trying to get his life together. I remember it well it was on a Sunday afternoon. He was on his way back to school with a friend. His friend was driving, and as they left, I gave the young man some gas money to make sure they had enough to get back. My son hugged and kissed me and said," see you later, ma" . I said in "two weeks. We'll get ready for the holidays when you get home". "Ok," he said. They drove off, and it was 2 hours later when I got a call that there had been an accident. They did not tell me exactly what happened but asked how soon I could get to the hospital. In my heart, I knew at that moment something was wrong. I could feel it in my bones.

I was too nervous to talk to anybody or even get anybody to come with me. I just had to get there. I got in my car, and I promised you as I drove; I don't remember seeing the highway. After riding for about 2 hours, I saw the sign to the hospital exit. I put on my blinkers and exited the interstate. When I got to the hospital, people were standing around outside. I didn't know them, so I immediately went to the desk, told the nurse who I was, and asked her what she could tell me about my son. The nurse looked at me and said I'll get the doctor for you.

I know it was only about 2 minutes, but it felt like two hours before I saw her coming back with a man following her. He extended his hand to me and said, my name is Dr. Collins. Will you please come with me we can talk in this office? I told Dr Collins, I don't mind talking, but can I see my son first? Is he hurt bad? He said "come with me, and we'll take care of everything." I followed him into that office, and I felt so strange I didn't recognize anything. Dr. Collins closes the door and says, "please be seated." I said, if you don't mind, I'll stand. He said" okay." Then he said "I don't know how to tell you this, but your son was involved in a severe accident this afternoon, it was a head-on collision, and he didn't make it; I'm sorry." I was silent for I don't know how long, finally the doctor asked me if I was ok? I didn't know how to answer that. He had told me that the center of my joy was gone, and now he's asking if I'm ok. Of course, I'm not okay. 'Where is my son?' I asked; 'I want to see him?' He then says, " I can arrange that but are you sure you want to?" 'Yes, I am' I said. He said," ok, stay here, and when we're ready, the nurse will come and get you." I sat there in a fog. People came in and inquired how I was, and I guess I said, ok, I don't know.

The nurse eventually returned to get me, and I made that lonely walk. We entered that room, and everything was so quiet, and my son was lying so still. Tears were flowing down my face as I got closer to the table. I stooped to kiss him and saw a cut on his face. I whispered, I love you, son. I walked out of that room as dead as I felt my son was. Somehow, we had a funeral over the next week and buried my son. You know it is strange how we grieve. As long as there were things to do, I kept moving, taking care of everything. Now when everything was over, my grief was worse. The people who had surrounded me before the funeral were all gone. I had nothing but time on my hand. So I slumped deeper and deeper into depression. I went to work and came home. I went to work and came home. I wasn't interacting with anyone. When people asked how I was doing, I said OK and went home to cry all night.

That went on for at least three months straight. One Saturday night, I was looking through our picture album. There was a picture of my son and me, and on the image, it said, No matter where we are, we will always be together. I began to cry again, but I didn't miss the picture's message. Even though my son was gone, there were parts of him that would always be with me. It took months, but I gradually felt myself melting and coming back to life. I decided to go back to church. I had not been for years. Even though I was hesitant, it proved to be just what I needed. I got involved in several ministries and enjoyed the work. It was about two years later that one Sunday Morning after service, as I was talking to one of the ladies, a young lady came up to me and asked if she could speak to me. I said sure; I thought she must need something from the teenage workers.

I turned to her, and I could see tears in her eyes. She said her name was Linda. I said, nice to meet you, Linda. She said," look, I'm just going to cut to the point. I knew your son Tim, and when he died, I was pregnant for him." I think for a moment my heart stopped beating. What are you talking about? My son didn't have a girlfriend.

"He may not have called me girlfriend, but we had sex several times.

Anyway, I have your grandson". My grandson, I have a grandson

"Yes, you do".

When can I see him?

"That's what I want to talk to you about. I'm only 20. I have no money and no help. I have struggled to raise him, but I can't do it." Tim has been dead for almost four years. Where have you been? Why didn't you contact me before.?

"I didn't think you would believe me. I had a job, and I could keep a roof over our heads. But a couple of weeks ago I lost my job. Last week I lost my apartment. I have lost my life with this child. I can't do anything; I don't have friends. I need help."

What can I do?

"Can you take him to stay with you for a while? Right now, we're homeless I'm sleeping on my friend's sofa. She wants us out."

I'm so sorry to hear that. You all can come to stay with me.

"I don't need to come. I just need you to take him. I have a job coming up, and I can't do it with a baby and no one to take care of him."

Of course, I'll help. I can watch him whenever you need me to.

"Ok, it would help if you did watch him. Could you keep him for a while? My job is in another city. I need to get settled, get a job, and a place for us. When I get set up, I'll come back and get him."

How long do you think that's going to be?

"I can't say exactly. But if you don't take him, I'll have to find a place for him."

What do you mean by a place?

""What I mean is if you don't take him, I will have to place him in the system, possibly with a foster family."

"A foster family?

Yes, I can't do anything else. I have no family. You're my last hope. Now can you take him? "

Yes, yes, I can.

Before I knew what was happening, she was gone. I was stunned. Later that day, she showed up at my housr with a beautiful toddler baby boy. When I looked at him, I saw my son because the child was his spitting image. She had a Walmart bag with a few pieces of clothing for him.

Where is the rest of his stuff? I asked if I could hold him, and she said," of course." I took him in my arms, and I knew from that moment that I was already in love with that baby. Before I could get comfortable, she said she had to go. Go where I said? She said "I have a job interview in the morning," so she had to go where she could get a ride. I knew something was up, but I couldn't say just what.. I asked where is his milk, his pampers.? She said "he likes mac and cheese." She turned toward the door to leave, and I said, when are you coming back? She said "in a couple of days." I said you're going to leave your baby for a couple of days. She said, "yes, you're his grandma, so I know he's in good hands." Again she turned to leave, and I asked, what's his name? You didn't tell me the baby's name. "Tim, I call him Little Tim." I didn't know it then, but that was the last time I saw her. That was 15 years ago. Standing there with a baby in my arms, I tried to figure out my next move. Remarkedly, the baby never cried. He sat on my sofa and went straight to sleep. I covered him with a blanket, and I sat there and watched him sleep. My mind went a thousand miles an hour. 2 hours later, when he woke up, we went to Walmart to buy his supplies and the rest is history. He's been with me ever since that day.

Marilyn ask. "Why didn't you tell us?"

'Because I felt that that was what God wanted me to do. I told people that I was raising my grandson. I never mentioned his mother, and after a while, no one asked. My grandson was a joy to me. I loved every moment. It was as if God had given me another chance.

But Ruth, that's a story with a happy ending, isn't it? Neomia ask

That's not the end of the story.

For the last year and a half, he has strayed away. Last year when he made 16, he started skipping classes. I was called to the school and told that he had been skipping classes. When they showed me his grades, he had failed most of his classes. I was shocked and embarrassed. When I got home and spoke to him, he said the school was stupid. I told him I didn't care how stupid the school was, he was going. That was just the beginning. A few weeks later, I got another call about him cutting school. The principal said he was hanging with the wrong crowd. He wouldn't tell me the other students' names, but he said it was a tough group. Once again, I spoke to Tim. This time he appeared to ignore every word I said. He turns to me and says, do what you want; I'm not going back to school. It's boring and a waste of time. He gets up while I'm still talking and walks out. He goes into his room and turns the music up as loud as possible. I knocked on the door, and he did not answer. I push the door open, and there he is, lying on the bed listening to music. I rushed to the outlet and pulled it out of the socket. The music goes off, and he jumps up." Why are you messing with my music" he says?

As long as you live with me, I say, we don't play music that way here. "It's my room so I can play what I want." No, Tim, you can't, my house, my rules.." So I don't live here anymore?" he asked me. That's your choice I said. But if you will follow my rules you can stay. I walked out of that room trembling; I was so upset. I felt like I was in the twilight zone. This child I had been raising since he was a baby I did not recognize. A few months ago, he was on the honor role, he was obedient, and I was very proud of him.

As time went on, it didn't get any better. Now that he is 17, I know he's smoking weed. I can smell it when he comes in. He doesn't even come home every night. When he's not there, I worry all night. The icing on the cake is that the police brought him home three nights ago. He was involved in some criminal activity. The only reason they let him come home was that one of the police officers went to church with us. The officer told him that he would be put in jail if he got involved with anything else. He's only a couple of days from his 18th birthday. Believe it or not, after the police left, I tried to talk to him. He slammed the door to his room and refused to come back out. I don't know what to do. I feel like such a failure

"Ruth, I am so sorry to hear this." Dora says "Please tell me, why are you blaming yourself? You didn't anything wrong."

I feel responsible. His dad is dead; his mother left him

Neomia takes her hand and says, "His mother may have left, but you didn't You gave that child everything. You can't second guess yourself like that. The Bible says train them up in the way you would have them go, and even if they stray, they will return grounded in that word you taught them."

I Know that is truth but still, I just don't know anymore. The relationship that my son and I had was so different. He would never have spoken to me in the way that he does.

Ruth, the one thing every mother knows is that every child is different. No two children act the same way. Stop looking at him as the personality and character of your son. Obviously, he is very different. It's time for you to stand back and see the salvation of God

Everything and everybody has a course that they must run. It's not always easy, but God knows just how much we can bear.

"Ruth has he ever hit you?" Marilyn asks

No, That's the only thing he has not done. He has put holes in my walls, stole my money, stole my car, sold some of my jewelry. Since nobody's ever there but me or him, I know he takes it

" So", Dora ask, " what is your plan?

That's the problem. I don't have a plan.

Are you going to let him run you out of your house? Are you willing to give up everything for him.? Mary asked?

Last week If you had asked that question, my answer may have been yes. Right now, my answer is no. God gave me this house. I'm not letting anyone take it over; I prayed about it. And that's the reason I wanted to talk to you all so that you could pray with and for me.

That is not a problem we can do that.

I prayed and asked the Lord for strength to go through this problem. His response was for me to be steadfast, unmovable, and abounding in his word. When I prayed that prayer, I had to give myself up; I had to put pride aside and walk worthy. I have already loosed it and let it go.' I told him last night that I was changing my locks this morning, and until he gets serious, don't worry about coming home. He looked at me and gave me a thumbs-up sign. Now I've put him in God's hands. I went to bed, and I slept soundly for the first time in 2 years.

That's what I'm talking about; if you are going to pray, don't worry. God promised to take care of you.

I know this problem will not disappear, but I feel that I got a handle.

Children can put you through some things

Dora stands and moves over to where Ruth was standing, "Ruth, you know I went through that with my son, started with drugs with his friends, started stealing, and ended in jail. I thought I was dying. My heart was broken, and I felt like I was the problem. I had to give it to Jesus. That's the only way I got through. You've got to put it in His hands.

I know I already have, but I feel much better now that I have shared it with you all. It feels like a load taken off my shoulder. I will continue to pray for him, but I can't take responsibility.

You remember what we said about pushing things under the rug, all you end up with is a lumpy rug. Issues must be confronted and dealt. Stop hiding behind pride.

The closer I get to God, the better he makes me feel. I've learned that the things and the people we love can make us take our eyes off Jesus and focus on the things of the world. We need a focused vision to stay with God.

Thank you for sharing. And Ruth, thank you for being a strong woman of God. Let's have a prayer and go on home. Everyone hold hands and pray for the hands you are holding. They prayed for a few minutes, and everyone left to go home."

As fate would have it Ruth did not have to wait long for something to happen. The next morning as she went to check her grandson's room, she found he had not come home. Upset but not defeated she prayed a prayer for him that he was ok. Later that morning the police were knocking on her door. After identifying themselves they told her that her grandson had been arrested in a robbery ring. He and some other guys were breaking into houses. He was being held in jail until bond was set.

Ruth did well until after the police left. She cried and cried, she prayed and prayed. Later she got up washed her face and accepted what had happened. In the weeks to come she went to court to see what the justice system would do with her grandson. Doing all that she could, at the end of the trial, he still got a year in jail. He got that because she convinced him to confess what he had done. Being his first serious crime, the judge had mercy on him, As she sat there looking at him she still wondered if there was something she should have done.

He was sent to jail not far from where she lived so she was able to visit him. It was very uncomfortable at first. He barely wanted to say a word to her. But as the weeks turned to months they had more and better conversations. While in jail he earned his GED. She told him how proud she was of him. Months after being there he finally apologized to her for his behavior for the last few years. He earnestly thanked her for putting up with him and promised to do better when he got out.

Three months later he was out but on probation. She allowed him to come and live with her and told him they would have to have some rules. He agreed. Months after being out of jail Ruth could tell that he was very different than the young man he was before. He had a job. Took care of his chores around the house but most of all everyday he continued to show his grandmother how much he appreciated her. It brought tears to Ruth's eyes. She had surely come full circle with him. She never missed and opportunity to thank God for all that he had done.

The ladies in her circle had stood by her side through it all. Giving her the support, she needed during those unbearable times.

Ruth got her breakthrough. Now, as Ruth thought about there was nothing, she could do but thank God for His Grace and Mercy. Nothing would ever make her stop loving her grandson. She would continue to pray for him, and watch God work in his life.

God should always remain #1 in our lives, even where our children are concerned. Remember even the strong women who appear so strong sometimes need to lean on someone.

Remember the Lord in everything you do, and he will show you the right way. Proverbs 3:6(GNT)

5

OUR DUTY (CHARGE)

E verything that you've read so far is true. For every story that has been shared there is at least fifty more like it. This small group of women is only a dot in the big picture of what's going on in the world. However, every act that was rendered I know was Blessed by God. You don't need millionaire status to do some good.

These women have and are making a difference in the lives of the women they touch. Every woman deserves to have someone that they can reach out to. There's a big need. So many hurt women, so much pain, but few who are willing to do something about it.

Some women want to help; but don't know what to do. Wanting to help is one thing but knowing how to do it is something else. How do you start? Most don't have enough money to start an organization. Nor do they have contacts or enough influence either. So, what can we do?

What can we do to start giving service to needed vessels?

It's simpler than you think. Here are a few simple tips to start you on your way:

- A Kind Word. Something that is always free and available. Sometimes it's just what someone needs.

- Prayer. Pray with and pray for others. Spending time on our knees is fuel for our journey.

- Study the Word- As we study the word, we develop the mind of Christ within ourselves. You will find yourself conforming more to his way and his way. We are most helpful when we are Christlike A key factor in the success of any journey is to spend more time in the Word and less time on the stories, Facebook, Twitter, TV and other distractions.

- Nothing happens by accident. Every experience God sends us through is a lesson for us. I know some women have a lot of pride and don't want anybody to know what they are going through. Our testimonies is a powerful tool in evangelism.

- Humble is the way. Why do you think Jesus washed the feet of his disciples? He was teaching them how to be humble. Humility will get you where pride can never take you.

- If you love God and His people you can never fail. For God is Love. Do all you do as unto the Lord.

The reality is you never know who you will meet. In a day's journey there are so many situations that scream for our attention. Which of those will be a time when you must minister? We don't know. When you find yourself in that situation you must be ready. Think on the following situations and ponder on what would you do or say.

- Like the mother on the street trying to take care of her children, going from man to man. She wouldn't talk to any woman because she said she knew what they would say and how they would act with her.

- Or the mother who was living in her car with her two children. Changing in the gas station pretending everything was OK

- What about the mother who works every day, barely making ends meet? Sometimes not eating to make sure her children have enough to eat. She didn't want to confide in anyone because she knew the first thing they would tell her was that you got a job help yourself.

The truth is we can recall a hundred stories about women we've known and some we've never met. Every woman deserves to have someone that they can talk to, even if all you have is a smile or a good Word.

- Or what about the teenager like the one that was introduced earlier in this book. The one who was on the street, disparaged by her own mother. The teenager who came back to say" I just came to say goodbye and to thank all of you for all of your help. The first time I walked in here, I was rude and bad-mannered. Still, you fed me and gave me money. When I came back a month later, you guys welcomed me with open arms. Now I'm on my way to live with my grandmother and a new start. I can't thank you all enough.

Without your help, I wouldn't have survived. Jesus Blessed ten lepers and only 1 came back to say thank you. You won't always get a Thank you.

So Many women feel they have nowhere to turn, no one to talk to, no one to share a word with, no one who has been their bridge over troubled water, no one who comforted them in their midnight hour; God has given each of us a mission, He defines that mission in Matthew 28: 19 & *20* Go ye therefore, and teach all nations, baptizing them in the name of the Father, and of the Son, and the Holy Ghost:

Teaching them to observe all things whatsoever I have commanded you: and, lo, I am with you always, even unto the end of the world.

The problem is you can't fulfill the mission if you have never accepted Christ as your savior. You can't complete your task if you don't have a personal relationship with him. You can't fulfill your assignment if you don't love one another.

We can't come together as sisters united in Christ unless we have accepted him as our Master and Lord of our lives. It's getting late in the evening, the sun is going down, but my sisters have a lot of work to do

Every Woman has a Testimony

Every Woman Can serve

Every Woman can carry out the great commission

Every woman has something to give

Don't cut yourself out

Maybe you're that woman who wants to help and doesn't know what to do. Perhaps you're the sister who needed the help, and no one was there to give it to you. Maybe you're going through something right now. God made you a woman after his own heart. With every beat of your heart, the blood of life flows through you. God has equipped you to reach out and help somebody.

Every woman can help somebody. It may be a word or a deed. We can change the world if we begin to love like Jesus.

Every one of us come short of the glory of God. I STAND WITH YOU whether you are a wife, mother, sister, friend, co-worker, employer, or co-laborer in Christ. I have nothing but love and concern for you. If you need me, call me; I promise to have a listening ear. Now is the time, and today is the day to stand together and be the women God wants us to be. I urge every woman to pledge to become your sister's keeper. Lend a helping hand whenever you can. Every Woman can Give a kind word, a sound Word, a caring word if you have a loving heart. We are better together I love you with the Love of God.

A journey we must make. But we don't have to make it by ourselves. I got all my sisters with me. Together we can change the world.